THE
FUNNIEST
BORO
QUOTES...
EVER!

Also available

THE
FUNNIEST
BORO
QUOTES...
EVER!

by Gordon Law

Printed in Europe and the USA
ISBN: 9798692979865
Imprint: Independently published

Photos courtesy of: Ivica Drusany/Shutterstock.com; daykung/Shutterstock.com

Contents

Introduction

"If you were on a rocket ship going to the moon, the man you would want sitting next to you would be Tony Mowbray," said former Middlesbrough manager Bruce Rioch of his captain.

The immortal statement recognising Mowbray's contribution during successive promotions under Rioch is probably the most memorable on Teesside.

Middlesbrough have had lots of characters who enjoyed a colourful sound bite and none more so than the flamboyant Malcolm Allison.

He may not have been the greatest of Boro managers but his controversial remarks in the Ayresome Park hotseat and later as a radio pundit make him one of the most entertaining.

When the acid-tongue of Gordon Strachan wasn't taking down a reporter with a stinging put-down, he'd provide journalists with a stream of humorous insights.

Steve McClaren was another who came out with some strange musings, Gareth Southgate showed he had a humorous side, while Jack Charlton always called a spade a spade.

The likes of David Wheater and Paul Gascoigne caused much hilarity in the dressing room, while Brian Clough was king of the quips.

Many of their foot-in-mouth moments and more can be found in this unique collection of funny Middlesbrough quotes and I hope you laugh as much reading this book as I did in compiling it.

Gordon Law

THE FUNNIEST BORO QUOTES... EVER!

GAME FOR A LAUGH

"I was a good kid and a likeable kid. It's not like I was an idiot or anything, even though I looked a bit like an idiot with my bleach blond dreadlocks in the cold north of England!"

Craig Johnston

"I'm not saying I will walk out after one game, but I would prefer to go back to Sardinia and be a life-saver on the beach than sit on the bench all the time."

Gianluca Festa

"I got one or two goals a season, give or take the odd 30."

Brian Clough

"The training methods at Middlesbrough are a quarter of a century out of date."
Massimo Maccarone

"I am a Libran and we like to procrastinate. That's what we do. We like to chill and see how things pan out."
Mark Viduka is unsure about his future

"I'm really upset at the way I left Rangers. Of course I have regrets, about the flute-playing and stuff, but there will be none of that on Teesside. The gaffer has promised to buy me a guitar."
Paul Gascoigne after signing for Boro

"It is a great honour that Real Madrid have set their sights on me – I play like [Arjen] Robben. I like to dribble with the ball, to go for goal and to look for one-on-one situations."

Adam Johnson rates himself highly

"It's the first I've heard of it."

Jason Euell on being told he was named as an ambassador for a deaf charity

"I may be desperate but I'm not that desperate."

Dean Windass on playing for the side of his father-in-law, North Ferriby United

"It's costing me a fortune because as well as the fares, I'm arriving late for training a few times. We have a deal where anyone who is late has to pay £50, so I've already written a cheque for £1,500 to see me through the season."

Paul Merson on his commute to training from his home in Hertfordshire

"I played my way into the side when I had a good training session the day before the derby match. I kicked a few of the lads and the manager saw that."

Lee Cattermole, aged 17, on how he was picked for his debut at Newcastle

"The very thought of walking into Ayresome Park at that time was like a Catholic walking into the Vatican."

Harold Shepherdson on signing for his hometown club in 1937

"I reckon we will be relegated, I'm almost certain of it."

Fabrizio Ravanelli, ever the optimist

Q: "What is the key to scoring goals?"

A: "I don't know. But if you've got it, can I have it back please?"

Danny Graham during a barren run

"I don't see how one kebab can be the difference between beating one or three men or running from box to box or scoring a goal."
Paul Gascoigne is confused about being left out of England's World Cup squad

"We had a lot of laughs. The one thing which really sticks out was the day that Micky Fenton got a brand new Jaguar. He was really proud of it and we thought, 'We'll fix him'. So the groundsman, Wilf Atkinson, and I got a pail of whitewash and painted it all over Micky's new car. Micky wasn't too pleased!"
Rolando Ugolini on the squad's antics during the 1950s

"Football is in my blood, but do I want to put myself in a world where I rely on players, get sacked after six games and not see my children grow up?"

Captain Gareth Southgate on management

"It was so freezing cold that I couldn't feel my feet – I had to put pieces of newspaper inside my boots to help warm them up."

Juninho

"Some people think that a football dressing room may be a stony ground for Christians but I think it's a brilliant place."

Alan Comfort

"At first Middlesbrough thought I was crap –
too mouthy, too awkward."
Brian Clough

"The plaster cast was due off at the hospital
today, but I was bored last night so I decided to
cut it off in the kitchen and I spiked myself."
Paul Gascoigne

"The football pitch is my arena and I fight to
rule it. It doesn't matter if I am fighting lions or
men, I feel like I am the gladiator! I love the film
starring Russell Crowe and I identify with him.
That is me up there."
Massimo Maccarone

"Young people have less respect for their elders and an 18-year-old footballer that has done f*ck-all can pick up 15 grand a week."

Gareth Southgate

"I've never wanted to leave. I'm here for the rest of my life, and hopefully after that as well."

Mark Schwarzer

"So I did in fact spend two-and-a-half years in the Middlesbrough car park practising skills. But if you spend four or five or six hours a day practising, you get better."

Craig Johnston on swerving incoming cars

"When we were in negotiations, they sent me a video of some of Middlesbrough's matches. I watched it and all I thought was, 'My God! How am I going to play there?' The ball was just being booted from one end to another... In fact, when I first arrived there were one or two whose technical ability wouldn't even have got them into Sao Paulo's youth team."

Juninho

"Publicity is not my strong suit. Some footballers like to see their name constantly in the headlines. I don't."

Brian Clough had a change of heart when he became a manager

"They had professors running the course. One of them told me that he wanted me to shoot at goal from a distance. The Portsmouth goalkeeper was in goal and I beat him and scored. The professor then came up to me and told me that I hadn't kicked the ball right."

Micky Fenton, the scorer of 162 goals for Middlesbrough, on boffins turning up at a Birmingham University coaching course

"Fighting terrorism is like being a goalkeeper. You can make a hundred brilliant saves but the only shot that people remember is the one that gets past you."

Paul Wilkinson

"We play, we lose. Hamil come off, Hamil no score. I am not happy here."

Hamilton Ricard is not enjoying his football

"I didn't play many games for Middlesbrough towards the end of the season, or at the start or in the middle."

Paul Gascoigne

"It certainly wasn't luck, and I don't mean that conceitedly 'cos you can't get lucky 40 times a year. You can get lucky five times, but not 40."

Brian Clough is modest about his Boro goalscoring achievements

"The most important thing is to get Rangers into the Premiership."

Paul Gascoigne forgets he has transferred to Middlesbrough

"It's very unlikely that a Boro player will be the league's top scorer. That is because of the way we play and the characteristics of our strikers."

Gaizka Mendieta puts down Mark Viduka, Jimmy-Floyd Hasselbaink and Yakubu

"If they can put a man on the moon then surely we can beat Chelsea."

Gareth Southgate

"I've been working with Bill Bethick and he has been telling me if I start to feel angry I should count down from 10 to one. It is helping, although I am young and still learning."

Emanuel Pogatetz on struggling to control his temper

"I used to get so cut up when results went against us. I used to feel murdered if we had been beaten on a Saturday."

Jamie Pollock gets a bit dramatic

"If I had not been a footballer, I would have been a doctor, or porn star."

Christian Karembeu

THE FUNNIEST BORO QUOTES... EVER!

CALLING THE SHOTS

"I taught him to say, 'One, two, three, skiing!'
The skiing would lighten his mood and take his
mind off his fury."
**Steve Harrison on keeping Austrian
defender Emanuel Pogatetz calm in training**

"I haven't seen him yet to say congratulations –
I think he is on an open-top bus in Redcar."
**Gareth Southgate on David Wheater's
call-up for England**

"If you were on a rocket ship going to the
moon, the man you would want sitting next to
you would be Tony Mowbray."
Bruce Rioch

"And as for you, you kangaroo, you can f*ck off right now. You're the worst player I've seen in my life."
Jack Charlton to a 15-year-old Craig Johnston who had flown from Australia to Middlesbrough for a trial

"I always knew the kangaroo would bounce back."
Charlton after Johnston was transferred to Liverpool five years later for a then-record fee of £570,000

"It's a war of nutrition."
John Neal on working with Stan Cummins

"You'll never make a footballer while ever your a*se points to the ground."

Jack Charlton to a young Craig Johnston

"He was like a cowered cat who had been smacked too many times... I used to shout – and you could hear me and everyone would laugh – 'Adama, Adama' all the time. I pulled him in one day and said to him, 'Adama, I actually woke up last night shouting Adama! and I'm really pleased it was a boy's name, not a girl's name, otherwise my wife would have killed me!'"

Tony Pulis on Adama Traore

"At the moment Abel is fighting his case elsewhere, hopefully it's positive. Next week we will have the results of his B-sample and something more positive."

Steve McClaren forgets about the use of the word "positive" when discussing Abel Xavier's failed drug test

Gareth Southgate: "Right, I'm the boss now. I know it's going to be awkward for a lot of you, but I don't want you to call me Gate anymore. From now on I want you to call me Boss or Gaffer."

Ray Parlour: "What about Big Nose?"

"There's nobody more serious than Gazza when he's got his committed head on."
Bryan Robson

"He's got lovely clean feet."
Tony Pulis on Ashley Fletcher

"Scott McDonald, the most intelligent man in the world, Stephen Hawking him. He knows everything. Every time you tell him something, he knows it, done it, seen it, been it, that's why we call him Stephen Hawking. That man can do anything!"
Gordon Strachan

"We had our meal at the training ground before leaving [to play Villa]. We came outside and there was no bus. So I said to the players, 'Where's Gascoigne?' No one knew and we couldn't get him on his mobile. Then Gazza turns up driving this bus – he'd taken it by himself into the village to put a bet on at the bookies! He then scraped the side of the bus and did £10,000 worth of damage."

Assistant manager Viv Anderson

"Sometimes, we attack and Adama [Traore] is nowhere near the box. I say, 'Adama, if you're 30 yards away, you might as well be in the stand with a hot dog and a beer'."

Aitor Karanka on Adama Traore

THE FUNNIEST BORO QUOTES... EVER!

FIELD OF DREAMS

THE FUNNIEST BORO QUOTES... EVER!

"This is a man's game – unless the FA wants us to walk out with handbags, wearing lipstick."
Paul Ince on his failed appeal against the red card he received for pushing Sunderland's Niall Quinn

"It's been so long since we've had a penalty, nobody knew who was taking it. We had forgotten where the spot was."
Steve McClaren

"I think he must have been p*ssed!"
Noel Whelan accuses referee Andy D'Urso of drunkenness after he awarded a free-kick that led to an Arsenal goal

"It wasn't going to be our day, on the night."

Bryan Robson mixes his football cliches after a League Cup defeat at Tranmere

"When we played at Derby that season, I had a vest under my shirt that had, 'Where's Emmo?' written on it. If I'd scored, I would have pulled it over my head and shown everyone."

Craig Hignett on Emerson going missing

"The players said afterwards they were better at penalties than me!"

Gareth Southgate after Boro defeat Bristol City on spot kicks in their FA Cup replay

"I've got to be very careful with what I say about the referee because I thought he was poor all game really."

Luke Young fails to hold his tongue

"Villa was disappointing. When you lose at home, it always feels much worse. It is like being burgled."

Gareth Southgate after Middlesbrough's 3-1 defeat to Aston Villa

"What did I call him at the time? Nothing I could really repeat."

Stewart Downing on Roberto Di Matteo's winner for Chelsea in the 1997 FA Cup final

"Ronaldo is a cheat, simple as that. How many times are we going to see it?"

Gareth Southgate on Cristiano Ronaldo winning a dubious penalty for Man United

"I'm too angry to even discuss it. It was diabolical, totally unprofessional and I am very, very angry about it."

Steve McClaren rages at Gianluca Festa after his red card for spitting at Kevin Phillips

"I look like I'm lazy, like Romario, but it's not the truth. I'm just playing a game with defenders. It's a tactical thing."

Afonso Alves

THE FUNNIEST BORO QUOTES... EVER!

"Everyone in football knows [Clinton] Morrison can be an arrogant idiot who is obviously looking for a bit of cheap publicity. If he can't make headlines by scoring goals, I suppose this is how he has to operate. He even has the audacity to have a plus sign between the one and nine on his shirt. I don't know what it means – it's probably the number of goals he's scored in the past five years."

Danny Mills has a spat with the Birmingham striker

"Derby have cheated to get a point out of the game. It's as simple as that."

Bryan Robson pulls no punches

"What is the world coming to when you get a red card and fined two weeks' wages for calling a grown man a w*nker? It's an adults' game, so what's wrong with a bit of industrial language in the workplace?"

Paul Gascoigne after getting sent off against Chelsea

"We were robbed. That is the second time this season that referee has ruined a game for me. He spoilt the night. I am almost speechless."

George Boateng on referee Rob Styles who awarded a controversial penalty which gave Man United an FA Cup replay

THE FUNNIEST BORO QUOTES... EVER!

BOARDROOM BANTER

"[The job] has its downs. It doesn't sound right this, but sometimes I get people accosting me in the toilets in Yarm if there's been a bad result!"

Keith Lamb

"You should see his boots. They're like something you hang from your car mirror."

Steve Gibson on Juninho

"[He will improve] when he gets rid of the naivety, the honesty and integrity and he becomes as sh*tty as all the rest."

Keith Lamb on Gareth Southgate

"With Ravanelli and Emerson, perhaps their brains were in their boots and their hearts in their wallets."

Steve Gibson

"Keith was lucky I'm calmer than some managers, as they might have taken a swing at him."

Gareth Southgate on being sacked by Keith Lamb

"It was an awkward meeting. I wasn't surprised to read that quote about wanting to hit me. He felt it was the wrong decision and let me know in no uncertain terms."

Keith Lamb on firing Gareth Southgate

"We are appalled at the decision and the entire process. How can nameless, faceless people on a commission decide that our genuine claim for equality and justice be dealt with in such a flippant manner? It is a disgraceful comment to suggest our claim was frivolous..."

Keith Lamb fumes after Jeremie Aliadiere's appeal against his red card was dismissed

"We have amateurs in charge of the professional game. We need professional people making decisions, not these silly little men. It's ridiculous to call our appeal frivolous and I'm absolutely furious."

Steve Gibson is also angry after the FA increase Aliadiere's ban to four games

"We spoke about it really and out of it came the fact that we wouldn't speak about it."

Terry Venables on his talks about a new contract with chairman Steve Gibson

"When someone writes crap or speaks on the radio – whether it's on Century or TalkSport or wherever – and speaks a load of sh*t I don't believe it. But the people out there do believe it and they say, 'If Bernie Slaven says it then it must be true, he's got the inside track at this football club'. Well, Bernie Slaven doesn't have any inside track at this football club and he never will have, unless he changes and who knows when that will happen."

Keith Lamb

"I've often looked at other people getting involved in games like that and thought, 'What a prat'. Perhaps I enjoyed it a little more than I should have but I was wrapped up in the occasion."

Steve Gibson on his celebrations after Boro won the Carling Cup in 2004

"An ICI foreman was almost certainly once on the shop floor. A bus inspector once drove a bus. But how many FA officials and club directors have ever been footballers?"

Brian Clough

"When we won he was fantastic. But when we were losing, he was not the sort of guy you wanted in the trenches. The first thing you would do was shoot him because you knew he would shoot you."

Steve Gibson on Fabrizio Ravanelli

"Our long-term aim is to make Middlesbrough synonymous with a good team rather than cooling towers and chemical plants. We're well on our way – even though Ruud Gullit had never heard of us when we contacted him last summer."

Steve Gibson

Q: "Is Middlesbrough still a club able to compete in the world of big transfer signings?"
A: "How big do you want? Mido's 6ft 3in!"
Keith Lamb

"What chances are English footballers getting at major clubs? Steve [McClaren] can only work with the tools he's given. The Liverpools and the Arsenals – what are they contributing at national level? If we're the last club to fly the flag of St George, we will. We're going to stay English."
Steve Gibson after two Aussies, an Austrian, a Argentinian, a Dutchman, a Nigerian and a Portuguese were named in Boro's starting XI

"Who on earth do Spurs think they are? They bleated away when Dimitar Berbatov left for Manchester United in the summer – but they sold at top dollar. Then they want to snatch other players for derisory offers and try to unsettle players. That is what has happened here. Their offer is a joke. Why would we sell our best players to our nearest rivals? Stewart is going nowhere."

Keith Lamb launches a tirade at Spurs after they put in a £6m bid for Stewart Downing

"25 years as chief executive was enough of a sentence for anyone. I didn't get off for good behaviour!"

Keith Lamb jokes after leaving his post

THE FUNNIEST BORO QUOTES... EVER!

PLAYER POWER

"[Being dropped] hasn't affected him. He's just too dopey and too thick to let things like that affect him."

Andrew Taylor on teammate David Wheater

"Alen didn't conform. In fact I have taken quite a liberty in using the words 'Alen' and 'conform' in the same sentence. They were complete strangers."

Gareth Southgate on Alen Boksic

"He was selfish in everything he did."

Craig Hignett on Fabrizio Ravanelli

"I call him 'One Chance Willie'. He's been getting chances this season and he's stuck them in every time he's got them."

Robbie Mustoe on his nickname for Noel Whelan

"Tony McAndrew would never settle for second best. He was always ready to put a boot up someone's a*se."

Billy Ashcroft

"Get the fat b*stard off!"

Willie Maddren repeats a fan's request for Alan Foggon to be subbed

"[Juninho] looks tiny and reminds me of jockey Frankie Dettori."

Alan Miller is horsing around

"Alan was affectionately known among the supporters as 'The Flying Pig', such was the excess weight he was carrying."

Willie Maddren on Alan Foggon

"He is mad about bananas. He has them in everything, even in his soup. If he reached into his pocket for a pen, he would probably pull out a banana."

Andy Townsend on Hamilton Ricard's diet

"David Wheater comes in with these autograph books and asks players to sign. I say, 'Go away, I'm your colleague now'."

George Boateng

"Meeting David Beckham... I might take my autograph book!"

David Wheater on his first call-up to the England squad

"So while we were having the photos taken for the suits and sunglasses, he decided to spit and throw a punch. I dived in, fists flying."

Neil Cox on a clash with Fabrizio Ravanelli

"I worked at Cargo Fleet at the time and used to turn up for training in my work clothes. When I got back to the dressing room afterwards, I couldn't find my clothes. Micky had pinned them to the ceiling. And my boots were fixed to the wooden floor with nails hammered through the soles."

Alan Peacock on Micky Fenton's pranks

"When we started the season, we didn't have a goalkeeper. Well, we did but I am truly very sorry for him as he was not for the top level. I don't remember his name, but honestly, honestly..."

Fabrizio Ravanelli doesn't rate Alan Miller or Gary Walsh

"Today Wimbledon very difficult, long ball, long ball, us we pass, pass, pass, pass, pass, pass, pass, cross goal, 1-0, Yarm 85, lager, beer, Macky Millers."

Alan Miller on Branco's team talk and plans for after the game

"The Brazilians had dodgy music taste, all samba stuff with little or no lyrics!"

Craig Hignett on the sounds played by Juninho and Emerson

"Massimo, I love him until I die."

Jimmy Floyd Hasselbaink on Massimo Maccarone

Paul Merson: "What have you got?"

Alan Moore: "What do you mean?"

Merson: "Well I've got the best outside right foot in the world, so what have you got?"

The Irishman didn't have much to say in this training ground banter

"It does grate that Super Al may have got a golden f*cking handshake. People have given Alen everything for years and he's done them. Done them proper."

Gareth Southgate on Croatian forward Alen Boksic

"Alan would trip over the ball nine times out of 10, but if you knocked it in front of him and let him gallop after it, he was brilliant."

John Craggs pays teammate Alan Foggon a compliment... we think

"I used to argue with Paul Ince all the time.... I get on alright with him, I just didn't agree with a lot of what he said!"

Brian Deane on Paul Ince

"A horrible man, a horrible man."

Alan Moore on Fabrizio Ravanelli

THE FUNNIEST BORO QUOTES... EVER!

MANAGING JUST FINE

"People say we are having no luck, but we are
– it's just all bad."
Gareth Southgate

"They made me do that when I signed for Real
Madrid... I did three and tucked the ball under
my arm! They are not my forte."
**New manager Jonathan Woodgate won't do
any keep-ups on the pitch this time**

"No, the chairman's call did not come at the
right time. I wanted to spend another year of
my life travelling around the world."
**Gordon Strachan on being unveiled as the
new Boro manager**

"There will not be any foreigners coming in this time, that's for sure. We have to add that wee bit of enthusiasm and knowledge."

Gordon Strachan wants to evoke a British bulldog spirit

"Everyone seems to think we will be the victims of an FA Cup upset – but then again I've been second favourite for the sack all season!"

Gareth Southgate

"I don't read the papers, I don't gamble, I don't even know what day it is."

Steve McClaren

John Neal: "Who's that bloke in the car park with the long, scruffy hair?"

Boro apprentices: "That's the kangaroo."

John Neal: "Is he any good?"

Boro apprentices: "No, he's crap! Well he's here from half past six in the morning and he's still here when we leave."

John Neal's first day at Boro watching Craig Johnston train in the car park

"All this 'breathe in and stabilise' stuff – the instructor never told us to breathe out again. So for two minutes, I was holding my breath. I nearly killed myself."

Gordon Strachan on taking Pilates classes after leaving Middlesbrough

Journalist: "Expecting any action, Gordon?"

Gordon Strachan: "You'd better ask my wife."

The manager was asked about potential transfers before the window shuts

"Every defeat hurts. You might think it doesn't, but you ask the family. You ask the dog."

Steve McClaren

"It's like a marriage. You want to do things in life but if you don't have anyone to share it with, then it's not as fulfilling."

Gareth Southgate wants the fans to turn up in their droves

"If you go to Millwall and stand on the bench (you get it). I had it at Newcastle, you get dog's abuse – the swearing and people saying things. You want to respond and say, 'Me and you, outside, now'. But imagine that!"

Steve McClaren

"In the public's mind, players win games and managers lose them."

Bryan Robson, player-manager

"[I won't be] boiling a bag of grass and strapping it to my thigh."

New manager Jonathan Woodgate on a bizarre Real Madrid injury cure

"We have a one-sided window looking over the players' gym from our physio room. It means we can keep an eye on them..."
Bryan Robson in Big Brother mode

"It's an impossible job and, by the way, I've recommended you for it!"
Jack Charlton to Willie Maddren after stepping down as caretaker boss

"I'd more or less retired in my own mind but I thought what an opportunity – eight games with nobody booing me!"
Neil Warnock on joining Boro, with fans barred from stadiums due to the coronavirus

"These are people with no friends... who spend 10 hours a day on the internet and have no one to talk to. The internet is a powerful tool. People are bringing down the government in Egypt by going on the internet, so it can be used for good. But three or four abusive idiots on a football message board do not speak for the majority."

Gordon Strachan

"The wife told me it looked as if I knew what I was doing a bit more."

Gareth Southgate explains why he switched from tracksuits to suits

"We are trying hard to bring in people who can lead... I want to bring in leaders and men – that's hugely important now. I have to have people who I know, players I know who are men, who are leaders."

Gordon Strachan won't be signing any followers or women

"I'm a normal bloke, but when you have such an ugly face as me then it's recognisable and everyone on Teesside seems to recognise it."

Tony Mowbray on returning to face Boro as Blackburn manager

Q: "Have you spoken to Barry Robson about what happened and what has been his response?"

Gordon Strachan: "Not interested."

Q: "You talk about the positives that could be taken, do you feel you created enough chances where you could have won this game or perhaps should have won this game?"

GS: "I think I said that in the previous answer."

Q: "Does it feel like, although you have gained a point, does it feel more like a defeat? What about yourself? Do you feel like you are under more pressure now?"

GS: "Every manager is under pressure."

Q: "How do you deal with that?"

GS: "Take drugs and drink and smoke and get through it that way."

The manager after a 2-2 draw with Portsmouth

"It was tongue in cheek and everyone knows it was tongue in cheek... I am kind of agnostic. There's either nothing there or there could be. If I go and meet my maker and I'm asked, 'What have you done wrong Gordon?' I have upset a few people on Radio Five for being sarcastic. If I'm told I can't be let in to heaven, then that's a bit unfair. I haven't really got a problem with that."

Gordon Strachan tells his critics they should lighten up after a backlash over his joke about drug use

"Is it April 1st?"

Gareth Southgate on the Premier League's proposal to take matches around the world

THE FUNNIEST BORO QUOTES... EVER!

TALKING BALLS

"Everyone knew him as 'Gate'. Though it was weird to start calling him 'gaffer'."

David Wheater on Gareth Southgate

"He called us Tweedle Dum and Tweedle Dee."

Dave Hodgson on John Neal's nickname for him and Mark Proctor

"Gordon Strachan arrived, with a Scottish accent. I didn't understand anything. I signed in Nice because I understood absolutely nothing of what he was telling me. I can't even say if it was good or not, if it was English or not. It lasted almost two months."

Didier Digard

"Without wanting to get myself into trouble, I would say that sticking with one manager over a long period is not always a good idea."

Gianluca Festa on the club staying loyal to Bryan Robson

"Gareth's more the talker and listens to people when they're speaking – but if you need a kick up the backside you'll get it."

Stewart Downing on Gareth Southgate booting rear ends

"He could never remember our names. He'd say, 'You there' or 'Thingy'."

David Armstrong on Jack Charlton

"He was just running up bills for drinks at hotels that he was not even staying in and expecting the club to pay."

Terry Cochrane on Malcolm Allison

"The cat's among the pigeons and meanwhile we're stuck in limbo."

Striker Bernie Slaven after Colin Todd's exit as manager

"In training, Jack would sometimes set the dogs on us!"

Stan Cummins on one of Jack Charlton's coaching methods

"I used to impersonate the manager Bob Dennison and one day he turned round and caught me. I think the writing was on the wall after that."

Rolando Ugolini

"Jack [Charlton] and I got on great, but we argued almost every day."

Stuart Boam

"Without doubt, Jack was the man who sorted me out."

Graeme Souness on Jack Charlton

"We used to call him 'Big Mal the Kiddies' Pal'."
Terry Cochrane on Malcolm Allison wanting to pick younger players

"John Craggs put him on his a*se, right in front of the TV cameras. Almost as soon as he hit the ground, Jack [Charlton] got up and ran after Craggsy, who thought he was joking. But he wasn't. Jack was going mental... shouting and screaming at him, and would not give up running. He must have chased him for 20 minutes, with the cameras filming the whole thing."
David Hodgson on Jack Charlton

"I don't know what qualities they saw in McClaren. I realised it at Middlesbrough and now I have had it confirmed. Him being named as England manager was a big surprise for me. What talents do they think he has?"

Gaizka Mendieta on Steve McClaren's appointment as England manager

"Only in England could a man with such limited abilities be made into the national coach. The ever-smiling McClaren is without doubt the most two-faced, false person I've had the misfortune to meet in football."

Massimo Maccarone

THE FUNNIEST BORO QUOTES... EVER!

OFF THE PITCH

"I didn't realise that the Boro team was so young. I think I was the only player with children. And everybody seemed to have blond hair, I thought I might have to dye my hair."

Mark Proctor

"Middlesbrough is not very nice. I've seen two nice girls in two years."

Szilard Nemeth

"The most vivid Christmas of all was the year I got the turkey leg. You see, I had a long wait for it. There were eight in the family and only two legs on the turkey."

Brian Clough on growing up in Middlesbrough

"The moment I saw Middlesbrough I felt it was a strange, terrible place. I had never seen anything quite like it."

Emerson

"I am doing the surfaces two to three times a day. I am paranoid about that. I wash my fruit with suds. I've not told her [wife Sharon] about me going round spraying everything because I don't want her thinking it is going to be the norm."

Neil Warnock on recovering from Covid-19

"I love the game – I fall out with the missus because I watch too much at home."

Jonathan Woodgate

"I'm not saying you have to be married to be a good footballer. I'm just saying it felt strange to come to a club where there are only three members of the first-team squad who are married. You need responsibility in life. I'm not going about finding wives for them, it was just a shock to me."

Gordon Strachan on a lack of commitment from his players

"Thank God it's only on match days we have to go into Middlesbrough. The place is an industrial town, pure and simple. I would not want to live in the town. All you've got there is smoking chimneys."

Emanuel Pogatetz

"We used to go to the pictures every Saturday night but we had to leave a little bit early and get home and watch Match of the Day. My wife still complains she missed the last five minutes of every film we saw."

Brian Clough

"I decided to come here because I like the shopping."

Mido on why he joined Middlesbrough

"Upon my boy's head, I never said English players are overweight, knackered and drunk."

Fabrizio Ravanelli is "misquoted" again in the Italian media

"My dad was a football fanatic and he worked in a sweet factory. What else does a boy need?"

Brian Clough recalls his childhood in Middlesbrough

"If I have any visitors, we always go to Newcastle, Leeds, or York. Middlesbrough is very bad. It is not a very nice town and there are a lot of factories."

Szilard Nemeth

"It was like moving from Butlin's to Belsen."

Brian Clough on relocating from Middlesbrough to Sunderland

"The other thing that bothers me is the way people seem to be against the French beef at the moment."

French star Christian Karembeu may not be enjoying life in England

"I'll tell you what my dream is. I mean my absolute number one dream that I will die happy if it happens – I want to see a UFO."

Paul Gascoigne

Head waiter: "Mr Allison, your bar bill – I have to tell you, it is enormous."

Malcolm Allison: "Is that all? You insult me. Don't come back until it's double that!"

"I have a little girl and I hope she never comes home with a professional footballer. Even the car insurance for footballers is expensive because the companies know they drive under the influence of alcohol."

George Boateng

"Most of the time I'm portrayed as an OK if pretty dull bloke. Then when I stick a paper bag over my head on national television and make an idiot of myself, people hammer me for not taking things seriously enough. You can't win!"

Gareth Southgate recalling that Pizza Hut ad after Euro 96

"On Saturdays, men would head to the match, then down the boozer and pick up some fish and chips on the way home. If they could manage it, there was probably a bit of rolling around in the bed with the wife and then snoring for 10 hours."

Brian Clough on life in Middlesbrough in the 1950s

"People from the club tried to be friendly. They invited us to eat but it was all this heavy food. And I couldn't understand anything they were saying."

Emerson's wife Andrea

Q: "Is your flashy image appropriate for the industrial North East?"

A: "That's not me, that's the press. They're always giving me cigars and taking pictures."

New Middlesbrough manager Malcolm Allison

"A proper moustache. It would have been at Middlesbrough [where I grew it]. It was fashionable and fortunately for me I could grow one. And fortunately for me I had naturally curly hair and I never permed it. I got lucky. In my youth fashion was about moustaches and curly hair."

Graeme Souness

"We went out on this celebration tour. I said, 'Come on Robbo, come on, me and you, let's have a drinking contest'. That's my biggest regret in life. Ask Curtis Fleming or Graham Kavanagh, they were witnesses. I woke up on the beach. The kids were building sandcastles around me."

John Hendrie after winning promotion

"You can go to nice restaurants but you can't beat fish and chips, can you? My girlfriend Stacey is the same. Of course she likes nice clothes but she isn't one who likes to go to posh restaurants. She goes where I go – I am the boss."

David Wheater

THE FUNNIEST BORO QUOTES... EVER!

"Lennie [Lawrence] had called a meeting and told us it was Bryan Robson [as new manager]. Jamie Pollock was straight up to the bookies, wasn't he! Jamie won a few bob, he did."

John Hendrie

"We used to play with smoke from the chimneys polluting the pitch. The pollution was so bad I didn't even send my son to school."

Fabrizio Ravanelli on his time at Boro

Q: "Are you feeling your age? What do you feel like?"

A: "I feel like a kebab and onions."

Paul Gascoigne

"I have not spoken with anyone regarding a move away from Middlesbrough, nor do I want to. My family is settled on Teesside. We're all very happy... I want the fans to know I'm not looking to move anywhere."

Christian Ziege

"For all my good feelings about Middlesbrough, I'd like to go to Liverpool."

Christian Ziege, two months later

"I eat what the locals eat. As for fish and chips, I've never heard of them. What are they?"

Afonso Alves

THE FUNNIEST BORO QUOTES... EVER!

PUNDIT PARADISE

"Middlesbrough keep flirting with relegation and if you keep walking past the barbers, eventually you'll get a haircut."

Paul Merson on Boro's relegation prospects

"A Ferrari without a garage."

Italian journalist Giancarlo Galavotti on Fabrizio Ravanelli at Boro's training ground

"Bryan Robson has certainly brought in the big names. But it is like going into a nightclub and getting off with a big blonde. The lads will say, 'Phwoar!'. But can you keep her?"

Bernie Slaven

"Asprilla has got the ball. He's going to score...
He's through... he's... he's f*cking scored. I
f*cking knew it!"

**Century Radio summariser Malcolm Allison
covering Boro's home match with Newcastle
which resulted in his suspension**

"That's a f*cking disgrace."

**Allison's view of a linesman's decision at
Coventry that cost him his Century Radio job**

"It's party! Party! Party! Everybody round my
house for a parmo!"

Alastair Brownlee

THE FUNNIEST BORO QUOTES... EVER!

"By trying to sign Peter Crouch, are Middlesbrough aiming too high?"

Jeff Stelling

"Get in yer big Aussie. Mark Schwarzer is the greatest Australian hero since Ned Kelly."

Century FM's Alastair Brownlee on the keeper's penalty save from Robbie Fowler

"I was staring at Middlesbrough keeper Mark Schwarzer from 12 yards, knowing that I had one kick to put us into Europe. He saved it. The f*cker saved it."

Robbie Fowler

"After a year in charge, we had not improved one iota – the football was average, away results were abysmal, the worst league position in 20 years and he still doesn't know his best team. It wasn't just on the field that Strachan let himself down, off the field during post-match interviews he became an embarrassment to himself, the club and the fans. He was arrogant, obnoxious, sarcastic, cutting and rude. He came across to me like a man who was on the borderline of insanity."

Bernie Slavin on Gordon Strachan's tenure

"Middlesbrough is the second greatest place to live in Britain! Behind Hartlepool."

Jeff Stelling

THE FUNNIEST BORO QUOTES... EVER!

"Goooaaaal Maaaassiiiimo Maaccaaaroneee...
Maccarone's header and Boro have stuck a
stake to the heart of Dracula's boys."
**Alastair Brownlee on Middlesbrough's
fightback against Steaua Bucharest**

"I'll bare my bum in Binns' window again if Boro
score more than 40 goals this season."
**Bernie Slaven – and he did just that in 1999
after Boro beat Man United**

"I don't really know what is happening Jeff!"
**Chris Kamara gets confused after David
Healy's equaliser for Fulham against Boro**

"Boro have lost games they should have won, and that's down to inexperience and not having enough experience."

Paul Merson

"Aliadiere – sadly, more syllables than goals this season."

Setanta commentator at Boro's clash with Newcastle

"Middlesbrough are withdrawing Maccarone the Italian, Nemeth the Slovakian and Stockdale the right back."

John Motson

THE FUNNIEST BORO QUOTES... EVER!

FAN FEVER

"One Job on Teesside, there's only one Job on Teesside. One Job on Teesside, there's only one Job on Teesside."

Striker Joseph-Desire Job gets his own song

"Steve McClaren came to town, riding on a pony. Sunderland have got Phil Babb, but we've got Maccarone."

Boro fans chuckle at their neighbours

"Wo-oh the Tony Mowbray. Wo-oh the Tony Mowbray. Wo-oh the Tony Mowbray. Arm's up, flag's up, you're offside!"

A popular chant in the 80s

Fan Fever

"Ohh, we're half way there. Ohh-ohh! Aliadiere!"

A remix of Bon Jovi's Living On A Prayer

"We've got Willie, Willie, Willie, Willie Whigham in our goal, in our goal."

The supporters love Willie Whigham

"Came for a parmo. You only came for a parmo. Came for a parmo. You only came for a parmo."

Sung to Newcastle fans

"Victor Valdes, he's won more than you."

A chant at Man City, referring to the Boro keeper's trophy haul while at Barcelona

"Sing when you're skiing, you only sing when you're skiing. Sing when you're skiing!"

Boro away at Sturm Graz in the UEFA Cup

"He came to us from PNE, Ledger. Ledger. He's better than John Terry, Ledger. Ledger. He takes the pain, he's got no shame. He heads the ball and we're off again, Sean St Ledger, the Boro's number 12!"

Sean St Ledger gets a nice ditty

"Small town in Scotland, you're just a small town in Scotland. Small town in Scotland. You're just a small town in Scotland!"

Sung at Newcastle supporters

"Your dad. You're not as good as your dad. You're not as good as your dad. You're not as good as your dad."

Chant at Leeds keeper Kasper Schmeichel

"Spit in a minute. He's gonna spit in a minute. Spit in a minute. He's gonna spit in a minute."

Bolton striker El Hadji Diouf had gobbed at a young Boro fan

"Sanli, Sanli Tuncay. He's the greatest Turk in history. Bought from Fenerbache, now he'll score a goal for you and me."

The Turkish star gets a song to the tune of The Flintstones

THE FUNNIEST BORO QUOTES... EVER!

Printed in Great Britain
by Amazon

12621153R00068